BABYLONIAN LEGEND

OF

THE FLOOD

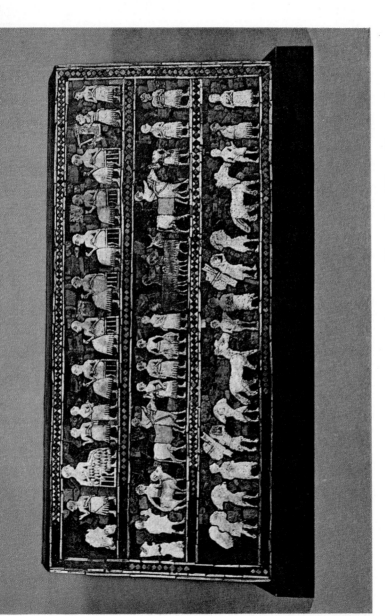

A royal banquet is in progress on the upper register of this scene, while on the middle and lower registers we see a procession of servants carrying precious gifts or driving asses and cattle. A similar spectacle might have been observed by Uta-napishtim's neighbours when he proceeded to load the 'ark' with all his possessions.

From the famous so-called 'Standard of Ur', a wooden structure decorated on four sides with scenes in coloured .... and .... inlaid in bitumen.—Sumerian art of the IInd quarter of the IIIrd

THE

BABYLONIAN LEGEND

OF

THE FLOOD

BY

EDMOND SOLLBERGER, D.LIT., F.B.A.

PUBLISHED FOR
THE TRUSTEES OF THE BRITISH MUSEUM
BY
BRITISH MUSEUM PUBLICATIONS LIMITED

© 1971 THE TRUSTEES OF THE BRITISH MUSEUM

First published 1962
Second edition 1966
Third edition 1971
Reprinted 1977, 1984

ISBN 0 7141 0777 9 *paper cover*

Published by British Museum Publications Ltd.,
46 Bloomsbury Street, London WC1B 3QQ

Printed in Great Britain
at the University Press, Oxford
by David Stanford
Printer to the University

CONTENTS

LIST OF ILLUSTRATIONS

PREFACE

This booklet is not concerned with the question whether there actually was a universal deluge destroying all but a few living creatures; nor does it seek to answer the much-too-often asked question, Is the Bible true? Its only aim is to present the reader with an account of a Flood story which has thrilled generation upon generation of Sumerians, Babylonians, and Assyrians, as well as their spiritual disciples and heirs, the peoples of Western Asia east, north, and west of the country which is now Iraq. This story is recorded in the cuneiform script, that oldest of all systems of writing, which for millennia was the great vehicle of civilization. Some of the clay tablets on which it was written were found at Nineveh in the course of excavations sponsored by the British Museum, and it is in the British Museum that a fragment of the story was first identified.

What we call *Babylonia* is the country covering roughly the southern half of Iraq from Baghdad to the Persian, or Basra, Gulf. Its capital city, from about the XIXth century B.C. to Alexander's conquest, was *Babylon*. The southern part of Babylonia is usually referred to as *Sumer*, her northern part as *Akkad*. The words *Sumerian* and *Akkadian* designate two peoples and two languages, whereas *Babylonian* is used to mean either both peoples and their common civilization (*Sumero-Akkadian* is also sometimes used in that sense), or the southern dialect of the Akkadian language. Its northern dialect would be *Assyrian*, spoken by the Assyrians in *Assyria*, the country which corresponds to Iraq north of Baghdad

[7]

and is the real *Mesopotamia* (a term often misleadingly applied to the whole of Iraq). Akkadian is a Semitic language cognate to Hebrew, Arabic, etc.; Sumerian, on the other hand, is an unclassified language which has so far resisted all attempts to relate it to any known living or dead language.

When quoting Sumerian and Akkadian words or names we have adopted a simplified spelling. The vowels should be given their Continental, or Latin, values (*a, e, i,* and *u* sounding approximately as the *u*'s in *buck, bury, business, bull; o* does not occur). Long vowels are marked by a circumflex. The consonants are as in English, *s* being always voiceless (as in *sit*), *g* always voiced (as in *give*), and *h* as the Scottish *ch* in *loch*.

POST-SCRIPT TO THE SECOND EDITION

Except for a few minor corrections (mainly misprints) and three additions to the bibliography (p. 30), the text of this edition is in every respect identical with that of the first, published in 1962.

It is worth reporting, however, that in the meantime a major discovery was made in the British Museum: Tablets I and III of the Old-Babylonian version of the *Epic of Atram-hasîs*, discussed on pp. 13 f. and 22 ff., have been found in the museum's collection of cuneiform tablets. Although the new tablets are damaged and incomplete, their importance cannot be over-estimated as they allow the reconstruction of virtually the whole text of the epic. Hand-copies of the new cuneiform texts have now been published in *Cuneiform Texts from Babylonian Tablets in the British Museum*, Part XLVI: 'Babylonian Literary Texts', by W. G. Lambert and A. R. Millard (London, 1965). A full edition of the epic by the two authors is expected in the near future.

NOTE TO THE THIRD EDITION

The edition and English translation of *Atram-hasîs*, referred to above, is now available (see Bibliography for details). Apart from a few additions to the Bibliography, the text of the present edition is identical with that of the previous one.

I

THE UNIVERSAL DELUGE

Most peoples on this earth have kept memories of a flood of such magnitude and disastrous consequences that popular imagination, stirred and amplified by poets, turned it into a universal catastrophe. As such, it had to be explained as a manifestation of supranatural, rather than natural, powers. There had to be a credible reason for such an unparalleled cataclysm and the most obvious one was man's wickedness and sins and his deserved punishment by the gods, or by God. Thus, flood stories are found in Asia—in India, Burma, China and Malaya, in Palestine and Mesopotamia; as well as in Australia and most of the Pacific Islands, and among the Indians of the Americas. They are rarer, though not unknown, in Europe as examples from Greece, Lithuania, Iceland, and even Wales would show. Africa, on the other hand, has apparently ignored them and it is indeed remarkable that the Nile Valley, where inundations are beneficial, does not seem to have produced any.

In our western world of Graeco-Roman, Judaeo-Christian civilization, the most popular flood legends are, quite naturally, the Biblical story and, perhaps in a more academic fashion, the Greek myth of Deucalion and Pyrrha.

All these stories, much as they may differ in detail, are built on a common pattern, the basic elements of which are: (*a*) mankind gravely offending the gods; (*b*) its punishment in the form of a universal flood meant to wipe it out; and (*c*) one just man and his family being spared so as to give birth to a new, better mankind.

But the very fact that Flood stories are found among peoples so diverse and so far apart, both in time and in space, shows that their common features cannot be but coincidences, being the product of the human mind's similar reactions to similar circumstances.

In the case of the Biblical Flood story, however, there can be no doubt that it is derived from a much earlier one. For when, in the troubled times that accompanied and followed the fall of the Sumero-Akkadian empire of the Third Dynasty of Ur (2170-2062 B.C.), Abraham's clan left Ur of the Chaldees in search of a new homeland, they did not only take with them their womenfolk and their servants and their cattle and other worldly possessions, but also the far more important riches of the Sumero-Akkadian culture and traditions, literary and religious, which were their heritage and would eventually influence and inspire the authors of the Biblical books. Among these traditions was that of the Flood.

2

THE REDISCOVERY OF THE FLOOD STORY

I

BEROSSUS

The first account of the Babylonian Flood in a European language was written in Greek, about 275 B.C., by Berossus, a priest of the great god Marduk, or Bêl, in Babylon, and a scholar. Berossus wrote a history of his country for which he was able to draw on an invaluable source of information—the numerous texts in the Sumerian and Akkadian tongues inscribed in the cuneiform script on the thousands of clay tablets which, no doubt, were at his disposal in the temple library. This work, dedicated to King Antiochus I (279-261 B.C.), was entitled *Babyloniaca*, or *Chaldaica*, and related in three books the long history of Babylonia from her very beginnings —the creation of the world—to her 'liberation' by Alexander.

As is often the case with ancient authors, however, we do not possess Berossus's history in its entirety but have to rely on more or less long excerpts as quoted or paraphrased, and sometimes garbled, by other historians such as Alexander Polyhistor, Abydenus, Eusebius, Syncellus, Josephus, or the Armenian Moses of Khoren.

The story of the Flood was told in the second book which opened with an account of the ten antediluvian kings of Babylonia.

II

THE RECENSION FROM NINEVEH

About twenty-two centuries after Berossus, a young Englishman, holding in his hands a fragment of a clay tablet which had just been cleaned for him, found that he was reading a narrative of the Flood in Assyrian: 'the first man', in his own words, 'to read that after more than two thousand years of oblivion'. 'Setting the tablet on the table, he jumped up and rushed about the room in a great state of excitement, and, to the astonishment of those present, began to undress himself!'[1]

George Smith, the hero of this story, by training a bank-note engraver and by vocation an Assyriologist, was a member of the small team of dedicated workers to whom the Trustees of the British Museum had set the formidable task of sorting, piecing together, and reading the innumerable fragments of cuneiform tablets found by Sir Henry Layard and others at Nineveh. He was convinced that a story of the Flood, earlier than the Biblical Deluge and confirming it, must be found among them, and he had indeed been on the look-out for it; nevertheless his excitement upon actually finding it was certainly understandable whatever we may think of his strange behaviour. Although his discovery was of far less importance, his reactions were similar to those of Archimedes on another famous occasion.

It was, however, a more dignified, and fully clad, George Smith who officially announced his findings in a paper read before the Society of Biblical Archaeology on the 3rd of December, 1872. It was published in the *Transactions* of the Society in July, 1873. Smith's startling revelations made such a sensation that the Proprietors of the *Daily Telegraph* promptly offered one thousand guineas in order to enable him to go to Nineveh and bring back more texts. The Trustees of the British Museum accepted the generous offer and granted Smith a six-month leave of absence. He thereupon travelled to Nineveh, resumed the excavations, and was soon finding new tablets (preserved today in the British Museum under the mark DT, for *Daily Telegraph*). Needless to say, they included further fragments of the Deluge story.

---

[1] E.A. W. Budge, *The Rise and Progress of Assyriology,* London, 1925, p. 153.

THE EARLY SEMITIC VERSION

As George Smith himself was perfectly aware, the text he had discovered was by no means *the* story of the Babylonian Flood but a rather late version of it. It belonged in fact, as Smith was the first to show, to that masterpiece of Sumero-Akkadian literature, the *Epic of Gilgamesh.* It makes up about two-thirds of the XIth tablet of the epic where Gilgamesh hears the story from the very mouth of its hero.

Smith was further convinced that 'his' text, which had been found in Assyria and could be dated to the VIIth century B.C., was based on earlier, Babylonian, versions which in turn were translations from an even earlier original written in the non-Semitic idiom of Babylonia, the language we now call Sumerian. These assumptions proved substantially correct.

It is now known that the original Babylonian (Semitic) Flood story was an integral part of another poem, the *Epic of Atram-hasis,* actually a history of Mankind. Although a large part of the work is lost—or, to be more accurate, as yet undiscovered—enough is preserved to allow for a reasonable reconstruction of the whole. This reconstruction has recently been proposed, with convincing arguments by the Danish Assyriologist Jørgen Læssøe in the journal *Bibliotheca Orientalis* (vol. XIII, 1956, pp. 90 ff.).

Of the numerous versions and editions of the poem which, no doubt, once existed, at least three have been recovered to date. Two of them are late, Neo-Assyrian versions (VIIth century B.C.), one in the Assyrian and the other in the Babylonian dialect. The third, earlier, version, the existence of which had been posited by George Smith, was written during the Old-Babylonian period: two out of its three tablets are indeed actually dated in the reign of King Ammî-saduqa of Babylon (1702-1682 B.C.). These two tablets are, respectively, the second and third of the epic and have been recognized as such ever since their publication by Albert T. Clay in 1922 (tablet II) and by Alfred Boissier in 1931 (tablet III). As for tablet I, although published by Theophilus G. Pinches, of the British Museum, as early as 1898, its connexion with the Atram-hasîs epic has only recently been established by Læssøe in the above-mentioned article. As Fate would have it, the three tablets, which Berossus may well have studied in his library, are now preserved in three different collections: the British Museum; the Yale University Library; and the Musée d'art et d'histoire at Geneva.

A further Old-Babylonian fragment of the Flood story whose connexion with the Atram-hasîs epic is however uncertain, was found in the Sumerian holy city of Nippur and published in 1910 by Hermann V. Hilprecht, professor of Assyriology at the University of Pennsylvania.

IV

THE SUMERIAN PROTOTYPE

In the year 1914, the Germano-American Sumerologist Arno Poebel published as No. 1 of his *Historical and Grammatical Texts* an Old-Babylonian tablet found during the University-of-Pennsylvania excavations at Nippur. Though most of the tablet is missing, the lower third only being preserved, it is of considerable importance. For here we have at last the text of the Sumerian version of the Creation and Flood story, the very prototype of the Babylonian *Epic of Atram-hasîs* which, with remarkable prescience, George Smith had assumed must exist.

With the possible exception of a small bilingual fragment from Nineveh which might belong to the Sumerian Atram-hasîs epic, the Philadelphia text is so far unique.

3

THE ACTORS OF THE DRAMA

The Flood story, as the description of the contents of its various recensions will show, is a highly dramatic narrative whose protagonists are gods and men.

I
THE GODS

En-lil, the son of An, the Heaven-God, and Ki, the Earth-Goddess, was the chief deity of the Sumero-Akkadian pantheon. Although technically under the leadership of his father, he played a far greater rôle in Babylonian life. When, for example, the gods had to decide on any point of policy, their Assembly would generally convene and one of them would propose it. The motion would be discussed, with the 'seven gods who determine Fate' taking part in the debate. The final decision would then be announced by An and En-lil, becoming their 'word' and thereby acquiring an irreversible power. It was En-lil's task to see the divine decision carried through. Thus En-lil, 'father of the gods', as he is sometimes called, ruled both heaven and earth.

He normally dwelt in Nippur, his city and, as such, the holy centre of the country, and it is only there and by him alone that the kingship of Sumer and Akkad could be conferred upon a king.

En-lil bears a Sumerian name in both the Sumerian and Akkadian traditions, the Akkadians never having felt the need of translating it into their own language. It means 'Lord Breath', the god being the life-giving wind: he created vegetation and the spade and the plough and, indeed, everything that is best in this world. But, being the god who loves, he is also the god who punishes, the destructive, hurricane wind. Gudea, a ruler of the Sumerian city-state of Lagash in the XXIInd century B.C., characteristically mentions the 'flood of En-lil'.

It is therefore not surprising that in all versions of the Babylonian Flood story he is the god credited with having convinced all the gods of the necessity of producing a Flood. All the gods, that is, with the exception of En-ki.

In the Sumero-Akkadian divine hierarchy, *En-ki*, another son of An, comes directly after En-lil. His name is usually interpreted literally as meaning 'Lord of the Earth'. This, however, hardly makes sense as En-ki is the god of the waters, especially of the sweet underground waters, and the name by which he is known to the Akkadians, *Ea*, might well be just another Sumerian pair of words meaning 'House of the Water'. On the other hand, his Sumerian name, En-ki, may possibly mean 'Lord Love'. En-ki is man's natural friend and protector, the god of wisdom, magic, and medicine. He has organized the world on behalf of En-lil—how could he let the world perish? He is the god of wisdom; he sees the folly of destroying mankind, thus depriving the gods of their servants and worshippers—how could he condone such foolish behaviour? It was only natural that his intervention in the Flood tragedy would be in favour of man. He could not repeal the 'word' of En-lil: that which the gods have commanded must be; he could, however, mitigate the terrible consequences of the Flood by rescuing one man to 'preserve the seed of mankind'. This he did with a cunning worthy of the sly Ulysses.

II

THE MEN

The Babylonian counterpart of the Biblical Noah, the just man who is spared the fate of wicked mankind, is called, in the Akkadian versions of the Flood story, *Uta-napishtim*. The name seems to mean 'I have found Life'. In the same Akkadian versions, he is also referred to as *Atram-hasîs*, an epithet meaning 'Exceedingly wise'. Now, in the Hellenistic tradition derived from Berossus, our man is called *Xisuthros*. This had been taken by the first scholars to deal with the Flood story (George Smith, the Frenchman Jules Oppert) as a mere Greek transliteration of the epithet Atra-hasîs with its components inverted into Hasîs-atra,[2] but Xisuthros is in fact a graecized form of the *Sumerian* name of the Flood hero, *Zi-u-sudra*. This name, the meaning of which, 'Life of long days', is reflected in the Akkadian 'I have found Life', is found not only in the Sumerian Flood story but also in other historical compositions.

Zi-u-sudra is listed as the last antediluvian king in the so-called Sumerian King-List, a catalogue of all the kings who reigned in Babylonia before and after the Flood. He is said to be the son of King Ubar-Tutu and is given a reign of 36,000 years, a not abnormal figure by antediluvian standards! His capital was Shurupak, a city which German excavations have identified with the site of Fara, some 95 miles south-east of Baghdad and 40 miles north-west of Ur as the crow flies. All this is consonant with the Flood story as told in the *Epic of Gilgamesh*, where Zi-u-sudra is addressed by the god Ea as 'Man of Shurupak, son of Ubar-Tutu'.

There is another man connected with the Flood story, though not directly with the Flood, and that is the hero *Gilgamesh* to whom Uta-napishtim relates his adventure.

The name Gilgamesh (or, in the Hellenistic tradition, *Gilgamos*) is an Akkadian rendering of a Sumerian name *Bilga-mes* meaning

---

[2] The absence or presence of the final *-m* is irrelevant, *atra* being simply a later form of the word *atram*.

'The Ancient is a Hero'. But Gilgamesh, or Bilga-mes, is not only a name, he is also a king, like Zi-u-sudra, and he too appears in the King-List: he is the 28th post-diluvian ruler and he reigned in Uruk for 126 years. The city of Uruk, on the present-day site of Warka in Southern Iraq, is none other than the Biblical Erech; there, the German team who since 1928 have been conducting extensive excavations on the site, found the earliest inscribed clay tablets ever to be discovered, roughly datable to 3100 B.C.

King Gilgamesh, who was later deified and whose cult is well documented—he was, for example, one of the favourite deities of the kings of Ur—is credited, among other things, with the building of the ramparts of his capital city, Uruk, and also with some important work on the temple-complex of Nippur, the spiritual capital of Sumer and Akkad. His heroic deeds and tall adventures were made the subject of a Sumerian epic cycle, comparable to our Arthurian tales, out of which eventually emerged the famous Babylonian *Epic of Gilgamesh*.

Although other texts make him a son of the goddess Nin-sun, and therefore of her husband Lugal-banda, the King-List tells us that he was the son of a *lillû*-demon, a sort of incubus. This tradition is reflected in a delightful story told by Aelian, a Roman writer of the late IInd century A.D. According to him, Seuechoros, king of the Babylonians, alarmed by prophecies that his grandson would deprive him of his realm, kept his daughter confined on the Acropolis so that she would know no man. But 'Fate outwitted the Babylonian'— the girl was made pregnant by 'an invisible, or undetected, man' and she gave birth to a boy. Her wardens, fearing the king's wrath, threw the boy from the Acropolis. He was seen by an eagle who flew underneath him so that he would fall on its back, and gently deposited him in an orchard. The gardener saw the pretty child, liked him, and reared him: he was Gilgamos and became king of the Babylonians.

Aelian had in fact incorporated in his story elements from other legends—the myth of Etana who flew into heaven on an eagle, and

[18]

that of King Sargon's origins—but some details are directly connected with the King-List. Gilgamos-Gilgamesh is the grandson of Seuechoros, a name undoubtedly to be identified with that of a Sumerian king, En-merkar. Now, if we go back to the King-List, we find that the kings of Uruk appear in this order: En-merkar; Lugal-banda, a shepherd; Dumu-zi, a fisherman; Gilgamesh. As already stated, we may infer from other sources that Gilgamesh was a son of Lugal-banda; the King-List shows how he could have been taken for En-merkar's grandson in the tradition followed by Aelian.

It is noteworthy that En-merkar's three successors were later deified—Lugal-banda as husband of the goddess Nin-sun, Dumu-zi as the famous god Tammuz, and Gilgamesh as one of the infernal judges.

4

THE BABYLONIAN FLOOD STORY

It remains to give an account of the different versions of the legend of the flood as recorded in the cuneiform script. Rather than complete translations, which could only be more or less verbatim transcripts of the numerous translations available (the more important will be listed in the bibliography at the end of this booklet), what is here given is a detailed analysis of the texts enlivened by some direct quotations. Those from the Gilgamesh version follow R. Campbell Thompson's beautiful rendering of the epic into English hexameters.

I

THE SUMERIAN FLOOD

The Sumerian legend of the flood is but a chapter of a general history of mankind. Unfortunately, it has come to us in a single, incomplete edition, the lower third only of the tablet on which it is written being preserved. Owing to the fact that cuneiform tablets are turned on their lower edge, and not on their left edge as are the pages of our books, we know neither the beginning nor the end of the text; just about one hundred lines, out of an estimated original three hundred, have survived. This, however, coupled with what we know of Sumerian literary style and mannerisms, is enough to help us get an idea of what was in the missing portions of the text.

The history, no doubt, opened with a description of the creation of the world, followed by the creation of man, the building of cities, and the establishment of kingship which came down on earth 'from above'. Parts of this section are in fact preserved, as are the names of the first five royal cities—Eridu, Bad-Tibira, Larak, Sippar, and Shurupak, each dedicated to a particular god or goddess.

In the lacuna that follows, the author must have described the behaviour of the people and how they incurred divine displeasure. Then we read of the gods' resolve to destroy mankind by bringing a Flood in spite of the opposition of some members of the august assembly. Inana, for instance, goddess of Love and War whom the Akkadians called Ishtar, 'the holy Inana wailed for her people'. As for En-ki, unable to prevail upon En-lil, he 'took counsel in his own heart'. There was a pious and god-fearing king, Zi-u-sudra, and he decided to save him. (Though the name of the merciful god is destroyed we may safely assume that it was En-ki.) Speaking through the reed-wall of the king's house, he tells him of the imminent catastrophe and (this in a new break in the text) how he is to build a boat in which he and his family will survive.

The text then went on with a relation of the terrible flood of which the end only is preserved:

'The mighty storm-winds, all of them, together, they rushed,
While the Flood sweeps over the . . . (cities?);
After for seven days, for seven nights
The Flood had swept over the land (*i.e.*, Sumer),
And the storm-winds had tossed the huge boat on the great
waters',

Utu, the Sun-god, appears, bringing back light. Zi-u-sudra prostrates himself before Utu and then sacrifices an ox and a sheep.

After a further break in the text, we find the gods recompensing the pious king, the 'preserver of the seed of mankind', by granting him eternal life as if he were one of them, and causing him to dwell in Dilmun 'the place where the Sun-god rises', which is now thought to be Bahrein in the Persian Gulf.

The remainder of the poem is lost.

[21]

THE EPIC OF ATRAM-HASÎS

Let us now examine the early Semitic version of the Flood found in the Old-Babylonian history of mankind inspired by the Sumerian composition we have just analysed.

It was the practice of the Babylonian scribes, when writing certain types of tablets, to add a final note on their contents. This custom, chiefly meant to help the Babylonian 'librarians', has proved invaluable to Assyriologists as it enables them to identify tablets, and often mere fragments, which otherwise would have remained unclassifiable. Thus, the colophon, as we call these notes, of the tablet referred to in section III of chapter 2 above as Tablet II of the Old-Babylonian epic of Atram-hasîs, reads:

'2nd tablet. When the gods man. Its total 439 (scil., lines). Hand of Ellit-Aya, the junior scribe. Month of Shabat, 28th day, year in which Ammî-saduqa, the king, built Fort-Ammî-saduqa, at the mouth of the Euphrates'.

It tells us not only the name of the scribe who wrote down this copy of the epic towards the end of the eleventh year of King Ammî-saduqa's reign (1692 B.C.), but also that this tablet, of which only some 50 lines are left, originally had no less than 439 and was the second of the composition which began with the words 'When the gods man'. Book-titles, as we know them, were not used in the ancient Near East where works were identified by simply quoting their first two or three opening words. 'When the gods man' or, in Akkadian, *inûma ilû awîlum* were therefore the first three words of Tablet I of the epic, both the beginning and end of which are now broken away.

Now, from the colophon of Tablet III, written by the same scribe Ellit-Aya a few months after he had completed Tablet II (month of A'yyar, 12th year of Ammî-saduqa's reign), we learn that it had 390 lines and was the third and last of the epic which consisted of 1,245 lines in all. Tablet I had therefore 416 lines. Out of the grand

[22]

total of 1,245 lines, however, hardly 170 are extant, in whole or in part, but nevertheless we still can obtain a fair idea of the contents of the epic. (In the following, passages enclosed in square brackets are supposed to have been in the lost parts of the tablets or are supplied by the Neo-Assyrian recensions of the poem.)

Tablet I.—[After the world had been created, the gods felt the need of having someone in charge of it.] They therefore asked the Mother-Goddess Mami, also called Nin-hursanga ('The Lady of the Mountain') or Nin-tu ('The Lady who gives Birth'), to create Lullu, the first man, so that he would 'bear the yoke' of this world. To fulfil the gods' wish, one minor god will be slain and his flesh and blood mixed with clay [out of which man will be fashioned. Mankind is thus born, cities are founded, kingship is established].

Tablet II.—But the population of the earth had become so numerous, and so noisy, that 'the god', that is to say En-lil, the chief deity, 'was upset by their uproar'. He called the Assembly of the gods and told them of his decision to punish men by sending famine, drought, and other plagues. [These having failed to reform man,] En-lil chose the supreme penalty: destruction of mankind by a Flood. [Some of the gods intervened in favour of man, prominent among them En-ki, the wise and friendly god who realized that En-lil's verdict was a double-edged sword—for how would the gods fare with no men left to provide them with sacrifices?] En-ki manages to persuade En-lil to let *him* command the Flood instead. [Thus he would be able to spare at least one man without En-lil's knowledge. He then goes to Atram-hasîs, the pious king of Shurupak, to warn him.]

Tablet III.—'Atram-hasîs opened his mouth and spoke to his lord', begging him to deliver his message. But En-ki cannot betray to a mortal the secrets of his fellow-gods, so he speaks instead to the reed-wall of Atram-hasîs's house. The king is thus duly warned to 'destroy the house, build a ship, despise goods, and keep the soul alive!' [The ship is built following En-ki's instructions. Atram-hasîs and his family go aboard with their craftsmen and possessions and

[23]

also 'beasts of the fields'. The Flood comes, destroying all of mankind except those who, thanks to En-ki's providence, had taken refuge on the ship.]

THE FLOOD AS TOLD TO GILGAMESH

Both early versions of the Deluge story have, as we just showed, survived in a badly mutilated text, so that to have a more detailed and complete account of the events of the Flood we must turn to that version of the story which is given in the *Epic of Gilgamesh*.

Known to the Babylonians under the 'title', *He who saw everything*, the epic was indeed a remarkable composition in twelve cantos incorporating with considerable skill several disconnected Sumerian tales about the king of Uruk, Gilgamesh, and his faithful friend Enkidu. After many a thrilling adventure, Enkidu dies and his death has such an effect on Gilgamesh that he starts on a quest of eternal life. The wisest course being apparently to interview the only man ever to have achieved it, Uta-napishtim, survivor of the Flood, Gilgamesh sets on a long journey, fraught with dangers, towards the place beyond the 'Waters of Death' where Uta-napishtim and his wife have been dwelling since the Flood.

Gilgamesh is reaching his destination in the last section of tablet X of the epic, so that when tablet XI opens we find him asking Uta-napishtim for the secret of his survival, a question the old man answers by telling him the story of the Flood.

As has often been observed by students of the poem, there is a rather important element wanting in this story: not a word is said of what had prompted the gods to take their fateful decision. Here, I think, we have but another proof of the author's skill. For whereas the earlier legends were part of historical works, namely the history of the world, in the Gilgamesh epic it serves an altogether different purpose. It is not an historical, scientific narrative, but simply the relation of an episode in Uta-napishtim's life as told by himself, a very old man, to a young king afraid of death. Therefore, the ultimate reasons for the Flood do not concern them, and it is fitting that Uta-napishtim's story would begin with the moment when he was personally involved, that is when Ea came to reveal to him the impending destruction of the world.

In the ancient city of Shurupak, says Uta-napishtim to Gilgamesh, the gods decided to produce the Flood. Ea however repeated their words to the reed-hut in which Uta-napishtim lived and, thus avoiding the guilt of revealing the gods' secret to a mere mortal, gave him his instructions. Uta-napishtim thereupon built a large ship according to the given plan.

This ship, or, as the Bible calls it, this 'ark', merely mentioned in the earlier versions, is here described in some detail. It was a perfect cube, the sides measuring 120 (Babylonian) cubits, or about 200 feet. The huge structure was divided into seven stories each divided into seven compartments. Enormous quantities of bitumen, pitch and oil were needed to make it watertight. There was a door and, at least, one window or hatch, and also probably a rudder since, as we shall see, a boatman was aboard. When the ark was launched, a very difficult job, two-thirds of the cube were under water.

Now, a cube, albeit perfect, is a rather strange design for a sea-worthy ship and Berossus as well as the authors of the Biblical account saw the difficulty. Berossus gives the dimensions as 5 stadia (about 3,000 feet) in length by 2 stadia (about 1,200 feet) in width; the Biblical ark was 300 (Hebrew) cubits in length by 50 in width by 30 in height, that is to say 450 feet by 75 by 45. Though still oversize, both Berossus's and the Biblical arks had better proportions than Uta-napishtim's. This does not mean that the Babylonians did not find 'their' ark awkward. They knew what a ship ought to look like, and the audience listening to the bards chanting the epic on the village square must have had the right reaction at hearing of the curious ship. But it had to be curious, since it was devised by the wise Ea, and as soon as they saw it, stranded on Mount Nisir, the gods did not for a second hesitate in guessing whose work it was. No sooner had En-lil asked how a man had escaped the Flood than they told him:

'O, who can there be to devise such a plan, except Ea? Surely, 'tis Ea is privy to ev'ry design'.

Having duly loaded the ark with his silver and his gold, his cattle, the 'beasts of the field' and the 'wild creatures of the field', Uta-napishtim led aboard his family and kin and all his craftsmen. At an agreed signal, he himself boarded the ship with his boatman, Puzur-Amurrû, shut the gate, and waited for the great cataclysm.

'(Then), when something of dawn had appear'd, from out the
horizon
Rose a cloud darkling; (lo), Adad (the storm-god) was
rumbling within it,
Shullat and Hanish were leading the vanguard, and coming
as heralds
Over the hills and the levels: (then) Irragal wrench'd out
the bollards;
Havoc Ninurta let loose as he came, th'Anunnaki their torches
Brandish'd, and shrivell'd the land with their flames;
[desolation from Adad
Stretch'd to (high) Heaven, (and) all that was bright was
[turn'd into darkness'.

. . .
'. . . O, were stricken with terror the gods at the Deluge,
Fleeing, they rose to the Heaven of Anu, and crouch'd in
the outskirts,
Cow'ring like curs were the gods (while) like to a woman in
travail
Ishtar did cry, she shrieking aloud, (e'en) the sweet-spoken
Lady . . .
. . . "Am I to give birth, unto (these) mine own people
Only to glut (with their bodies) the Sea as though they were
fish-spawn?" '

[26]

. . .

'Six days, a se'ennight the hurricane, deluge, (and) tempest
                                                    continued
Sweeping the land: when the seventh day came were
                                            quelléd the warfare,
Tempest (and) deluge which like to an army embattail'd
                                                were fighting.
Lull'd was the sea, (all) spent was the gale, assuaged was
                                                    the deluge,
(So) did I look on the day; (lo), sound was (all) still'd; and
                                                    all human
Back to (its) clay was return'd, and fen was level with
                                                    roof-tree'.

The ark had stopped on Mount Nisir, now identified with Pir
Omar Gudrun, or Pir-i-Mukurun, a mountain 8,600 feet high east
of the Tigris in the Lesser-Zab Basin. Uta-napishtim waited for
another seven days and then, as was indeed the practice current
among sailors in Antiquity, let out birds to reconnoitre the ground:
first a dove which, finding no resting place, came back; then a
swallow which came back too; and finally a raven which did not
return. Interpreting this as a sure sign that the waters had abated
and disembarking was possible, Uta-napishtim offered a thanks-
giving sacrifice:

'The gods smelt the savour, the gods the sweet savour
Smelt; (aye), the gods did assemble like flies o'er him making
                                            [the off'ring'.

The great goddess Ishtar, swearing never to forget the dreadful
event, urged the other gods to prevent En-lil from sharing in the
sacrifice since he was responsible for the catastrophe. En-lil, however, soon arrived and, seeing that a man had escaped, filled with
wrath, called for an explanation. Ea then

'Answer'd and spake unto En-lil, the warrior, saying: "O
                                                    chieftain
Thou of the gods, thou warrior! How, forsooth, how (all)
                                                    uncounsell'd

[27]

Couldst thou a deluge bring on? (Aye), visit his sin on the
sinner,

Visit his guilt on the guilty, (but) O, have mercy, that (thereby)
He shall not be cut off; be clement, that he may not perish.
O, instead of thy making a flood, let a lion come, man to
diminish;

O, instead of thy making a flood, let a jackal come, man to
diminish;

O, instead of thy making a flood, let a famine occur, that
the country

May be devour'd; instead of thy making a flood, let the
Plague-god

Come and the people o'erwhelm;
Sooth, indeed 'twas not I of the Great Gods the secret
revealéd,

(But) to th' Abounding in Wisdom vouchsafed I a dream,
and (in this wise)

He of the gods heard the secret. Deliberate, now, on his
counsel".'

Apparently convinced of his error and of the wrong he had done,
En-lil went aboard the ship, took Uta-napishtim and his wife by the
hand and made them kneel before him. Touching their foreheads,
he blessed them, saying:

'Uta-napishtim hath hitherto only been mortal,
Now, indeed, Uta-napishtim and (also) his wife shall be equal
Like to us gods; in the distance afar at the mouth of the rivers
Uta-napishtim shall dwell'.

As for Gilgamesh, who had travelled such a long distance to find
a way of escaping man's common destiny, Uta-napishtim tells him
of a certain plant which gives man eternal life. Gilgamesh eventually
finds it but as, on his way home, he is bathing in a stream, a serpent
comes out of the water and takes it away. Death, not eternal life, is
the lot of man.

A SHORT BIBLIOGRAPHY

1. On the *Flood* in general, and the world-wide distribution of Flood stories, the reader is referred to W. L. WADLE's article, 'Deluge', in the *Encyclopaedia Britannica*, 1960 edition, and A. PARROT's article, 'Flood (in religion and myth)', in the 1970 edition.

   For the *Babylonian Flood*, see—

   E. A. W. BUDGE, *The Babylonian Story of the Deluge and the Epic of Gilgamesh*, London (British Museum), 1920.

   A. PARROT, *The Flood and Noah's Ark*. 'Studies in Biblical Archaeology', No. 1, London, 1955.

   Chapter IV ('The Story of the Flood') of A. HEIDEL's *The Gilgamesh Epic and Old Testament Parallels*, Chicago, 1946, pp. 224–269. (2nd ed., Chicago, 1949; paper-back ed., Chicago, 1963.)

   M. E. L. MALLOWAN, 'Noah's Flood Reconsidered', in *Iraq* 26 (1964), pp. 62–82.

2. The more recent *translations* of the Babylonian Flood texts will be found in the following books—

A. *The Sumerian Version:*

   A. HEIDEL, *The Gilgamesh Epic* . . ., pp. 102–105.

   S. N. KRAMER, in *Ancient Near Eastern Texts Relating to the Old Testament*, edited by J. B. PRITCHARD, 3rd edition, Princeton, 1969, pp. 42–44.

   M. CIVIL, in LAMBERT & MILLARD, *Atra-ḫasīs* . . ., pp. 138–145.

B. *The Atram-ḥasîs Version:*

Tablet I (not yet recognized as such)—

A. HEIDEL, *The Babylonian Genesis*, 2nd edition, Chicago, 1951, pp. 66–67. (Paper-back edition, Chicago, 1963.)

E. A. SPEISER, in *Ancient Near Eastern Texts* . . ., pp. 99–100.

Tablets II-III—

A. HEIDEL, *The Gilgamesh Epic* . . ., pp. 106–116.

E. A. SPEISER, in *Ancient Near Eastern Texts* . . ., pp. 104–106, with additions by A. K. GRAYSON, pp. 512–514.

The complete text—

W. G. LAMBERT & A. R. MILLARD, *Atra-ḥasīs. The Babylonian Story of the Flood*, Oxford, 1969.

C. *The Gilgamesh Version:*

R. CAMPBELL THOMPSON, *The Epic of Gilgamish*, London, 1928 (Tablet XI = pp. 49–56).

A. HEIDEL, *The Gilgamesh Epic* . . . (Tablet XI = pp. 80–93).

E. A. SPEISER, in *Ancient Near Eastern Texts* . . ., pp. 72–99 Tablet XI = pp. 93–97).

J. V. KINNIER WILSON, in *Documents from Old Testament Times*, edited by D. WINTON THOMAS, London, 1958, pp. 17–26.

D. A translation of the *Berossus Version* appears in A. HEIDEL, *The Gilgamesh Epic* . . ., pp. 116–119 ; and in LAMBERT & MILLARD, *Atra-ḥasīs* . . ., pp. 134–137.

3. As for the *general background* of Sumero-Akkadian civilization, the interested reader is advised to read—

E. CHIERA, *They Wrote on Clay. The Babylonian Tablets Speak Today*, Chicago, 1938.

S. N. KRAMER, *Sumerian Mythology. A Study of Spiritual and Literary Achievement in the Third Millennium B.C.*, Philadelphia, 1944.

H. Frankfort, et al., *Before Philosophy*, London, 1949.
(This is a Pelican edition of 'The Intellectual Adventure
of Ancient Man*, Chicago, 1946. The chapter on
Mesopotamia [pp. 137–234] is by Th. Jacobsen.)

S. N. Kramer, *History Begins at Sumer*, London, 1959.

H. W. F. Saggs, *The Greatness that was Babylon*, London,
1962.

S. N. Kramer, *The Sumerians: Their History, Culture and
Character*, Chicago and London, 1963.

A. L. Oppenheim, *Ancient Mesopotamia: Portrait of a
Dead Civilization*, Chicago and London, 1964.

S. N. Kramer, *Cradle of Civilization*. 'Great Ages of Man',
Time–Life Books, New York, 1967.

Fig. 1. Two priests, predecessors of Berossus by five or six centuries, performing a religious ceremony before a shrine. The emblem on the crouching dragon is that of the god Marduk, the national god of Babylon. A female deity standing on a dragon as well as diverse divine symbols are seen in the background.

Chalcedony cylinder seal of Assyrian style, IXth–VIIIth century B.C.— Length 35 mm., diameter 16 mm.—B.M. 18249.

Fig. 2. Obverse of one of the fragments of the XIth tablet of the Epic of Gilga-mesh *in which George Smith recognized a version of the Babylonian Flood story. It belonged to King Ashurbanipal's library at Nineveh (VIIth century B.C.)*
Clay tablet.—137 × 130 mm.—K. 3375.

[34]

Fig. 3. Reverse of the Gilgamesh Flood tablet illustrated in Fig. 2.

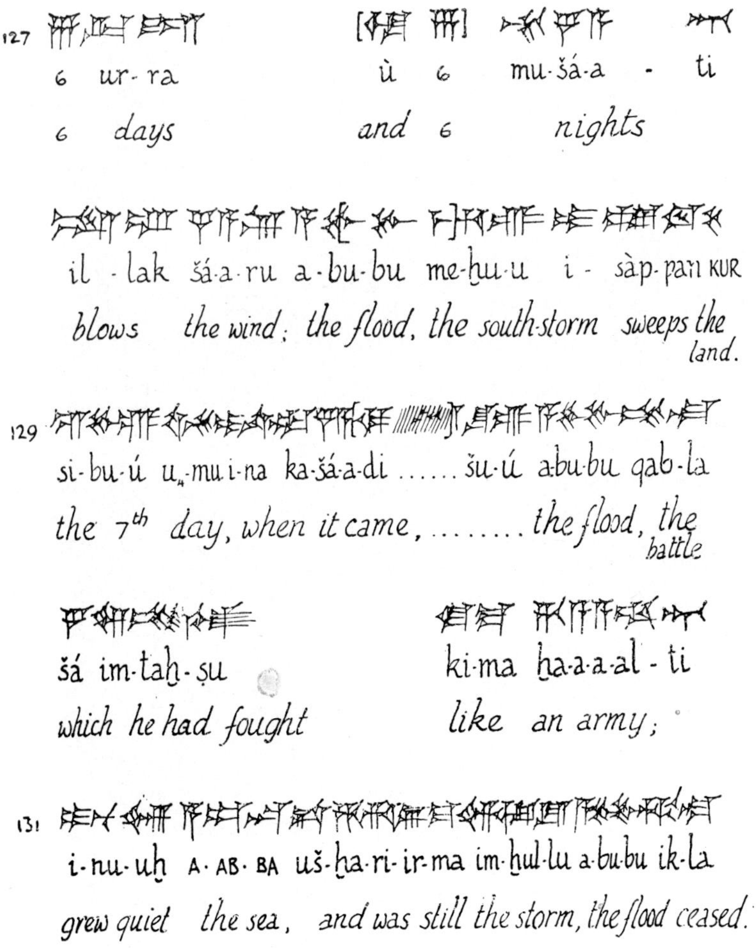

127 6 ur·ra   [ù 6] mu·ša·a - ti

6 days   and 6   nights

il·lak ša·a·ru a·bu·bu me·ḫu·u i - sàp·pan KUR

blows the wind; the flood, the south-storm sweeps the land.

129 si·bu·ú u„·mu i·na ka·ša·a·di ...... šu·ú a·bu·bu qab·la

the 7th day, when it came, ... the flood, the battle

šá im·taḫ·ṣu   ki·ma ḫa·a·a·al - ti

which he had fought   like an army;

131 i·nu·uḫ A·AB·BA uš·ḫa·ri·ir·ma im·ḫul·lu a·bu·bu ik·la

grew quiet the sea, and was still the storm, the flood ceased.

Fig. 4. Hand-copy, transliteration and word-for-word translation of lines 127–131 of the XIth tablet of the Epic of Gilgamesh. The text is that of tablet K. 3375 published here as Figs. 2 and 3. Passages in brackets [ ] are broken or damaged on the original.

Fig. 5. One of the Daily Telegraph *tablets found by George Smith at Nineveh, giving another fragment of the Flood story. The name of Atram-hasîs appears, in part, in line 11.*

Clay tablet, VIIth century B.C.—35×46 mm.—DT. 42.

Fig. 6. A Sumerian reed-house, similar to that of Uta-napishtim. The example shown here is actually a byre but any house would have looked exactly like this. The same type of house is—or, until very recently, was—still in use in some districts of Southern Iraq.

The illustration is a detail of the relief decoration of a stone trough of the Jemdet-Nasr period (2900–2800 B.C.), found at Uruk.—The dimensions of the trough are 1030 mm. in length by 380 mm. in width by 163 mm. in height. —B.M. 120000.

Fig. 7. *In front of a reed-house, probably a temple or chapel, a pig-tailed woman sits on a stool, both hands raised in a ritual gesture of worship. Several symbols and objects (a spouted jar, etc.) serve as filling motifs.*

Grey-limestone cylinder seal of the Jemdet-Nasr period (2900–2800 B.C.).— Length 17 mm., diameter 15 mm.—B.M. 123280.

Fig. 8. A Sumerian boat with passenger and boatman. Boats of this type are still in use in Southern Iraq.

Mottled-green jasper cylinder seal of the Early-Dynastic period (IIIrd quarter of the IIIrd millennium B.C.).—Length 30 mm., diameter 18 mm.— B.M. 89588.

[40]

Fig. 9. A hunting scene in the swamps of Sumer. While one of the two men is steering the boat, his companion is aiming his spear at a wild boar fleeing into the reeds of the swamp.

Stone bowl decorated in low relief. From Uruk; Jemdet-Nasr period (2900– 2800 B.C.).—Height 70 mm., diameter 158 mm.—B.M. 118466.

Fig. 10. One of the scenes usually thought to represent Gilgamesh and Enkidu. Should this interpretation be correct, we would have here the famous hero and his friend (shown as a bull-man, which is not supported by the text of the epic) fighting against the heavenly Bull. The episode is told in the VIth tablet of the epic. The group on the right ('Gilgamesh' fighting a lion) is there for reasons of symmetry. The small ibex under the (destroyed) inscription is a filling motif.

Green-jasper cylinder seal of the Early-Dynastic period (IIIrd quarter of the IIIrd millennium B.C.).—Length 40 mm., diameter 27 mm.—B.M. 89111.

Fig. 11. An interceding goddess (Lama). Thus might Ishtar have stood before En-lil, pleading in favour of mankind.
Terra-cotta plaque of the Old-Babylonian period (Ist half of the IInd millennium B.C.).—130×55 mm.—B.M. 127497.

Fig. 12. Sacrificial ceremony, such as Uta-napishtim might have performed after the Flood. On the upper register, a priest pours a libation in front of a seated god; he is accompanied by three female attendants. On the lower register, the priest pours a libation before the door of a temple or chapel. A male attendant, carrying a kid for the sacrifice, and flanked by two women, stands behind him.

Limestone plaque carved in low relief, found in the temple of the goddess Nin-gal at Ur. Early-Dynastic period (IIIrd quarter of the IIIrd millennium B.C.).—260×220 mm.—B.M. 118561.

Fig. 13. A map of the world drawn by a scribe on a tablet dating from the IInd quarter of the Ist millennium B.C. The upper rectangle represents Babylon while the lower one shows the marshland of Southern Babylonia through which the Tigris and Euphrates flow into the Persian Gulf. The Gulf is drawn as a river encircling the world and called the 'River of Brackish Waters'. There were some mysterious regions beyond these waters (the triangles on the map), such as the place where Uta-napishtim lived his post-diluvian eternal life. The name of the Flood hero actually occurs in the text.

Clay tablet.—122×82 mm.—B.M. 92687.

Fig. 14. A completely excavated pit at Ur (Joint Expedition of the British Museum and the University of Pennsylvania Museum). The floor is of the Jemdet-Nasr period (2900–2800 B.C.). The square opening at the foot of the stairs leads into the 'Flood deposit'. See Fig 15.

Fig. 15. A cut through the floor of the pit shown on Fig 14. The lighter-coloured stratum is the 'Flood deposit'; the darker stratum below consists of black organic soil containing potsherds.

It was Sir Leonard Woolley's contention that the 'Flood deposit' he had uncovered at Ur was the material remains of the Universal Flood. Similar deposits have, however, been found on other sites, and the dates do not always concur. It is much safer to assume that we have traces of local, violent floods rather than a concrete proof of the highly hypothetic Universal Deluge.

[47]